GW01090444

Drawings by John Olday

THE MARCH TO DEATH

a book of anti-war cartoons
first published at the height of the war
in May 1943

FREEDOM PRESS

© Freedom Press 1943, 1995

First published May 1943
Reprinted 1943
This edition published May 1995

ISBN 0 900384 80 8

Freedom Press
(in Angel Alley)
84b Whitechapel High Street
London E1 7QR

Typeset and printed by
Aldgate Press, London E1

Introduction to the 1995 edition

This book has two authors, one of them anonymous. John Olday did the drawings. Marie Louise Berneri, whose name does not appear in the first edition, selected the quotations and discussed with John Olday what he should draw.

All those associated with Freedom Press at the time were fervently anti-Nazi. They opposed the regimentation of society, the relentless propaganda, the way the elite profited from the armaments trade, while the poor suffered the worst of the war. These features were characteristic, not only of Nazi Germany, but of all the belligerent states on both sides of the war, so Freedom Press opposed them all.

The initial print run of 5,000 copies was sold out in a few months, and 5,000 more were sold by the end of the war. Philip Sansom and Laurie Hislam toured the country offering it (with other Freedom Press literature) to bookshops, who were pleased to take anything which would fill up their half empty shelves.

Probably not many of those who bought the book agreed that all governments are equally bad. For one thing, the British government permitted the publication and sale of *The March to Death*, which would not have been possible in Germany, Italy, Japan or the Soviet Union. But the book gave expression to the widespread dissatisfaction with the old social order, which was to find expression in the landslide Labour election victories two years later.

The drawing on page 19 must be seen in the context of its time, otherwise it may be misunderstood by hindsight as equating systematic genocide with mere oppression.

We have known *since 1945* that the Nazi genocide industry was unique in history. Other incidents of genocide and "ethnic cleansing" have occurred before and since, but only the Nazis had purpose-built killing factories, served by purposefully scheduled train timetables, for the purpose of exterminating an ethnic group.

But *in 1943* this was not known. The "final solution of the jewish problem" was not even planned before 1942, and there had been no information from Germany since 1939. Nobody in Britain knew even about the rudimentary death camps, where people were left to die of starvation and disease. The efficient gas houses and incinerators of Auschwitz were not even imagined.

In April 1945, when invading British troops came across the rudimentary death camp at Belsen, everyone was surprised and horrified. Gilbert Murry, who had edited *Peace News* throughout the war, decided in the light of Belsen that his opposition to the war had been mistaken, and resigned. The whole anti-war movement went quiet for three months, until the atom bomb was dropped on Hiroshima, and our confidence that all governments are bastards was restored. (The fact that about a million German prisoners of war died of starvation and disease was not known until decades later.)

The cartoon on page 19 is about what was known of the condition of German jews in 1943, namely their condition in 1939. They were not recognized as citizens, not allowed to own property, forced to live in ghettos, subject to all sorts of ill treatment, including murder. The condition of negroes in some American states may not have been exactly similar, but the comparison was fair.

Some drawings include caricatures of individuals who may be unfamiliar to young readers in 1995. This is who they were in 1943.

Attlee, Clement page 53. Labour politician. Leader of the Opposition 1935-39. Deputy Prime Minister in the war government.

Beaverbrook, Lord page 53. (Max Aitken) Canadian proprietor of the *Daily Express*. Political ally of Churchill.

Bevin, Ernest page 53. Started work on the docks aged 13. General Secretary of the Transport and General Workers Union 1921-40, known as "the dockers' KC". Minister of Labour and National Service in the war government.

Churchill, Winston pages 9, 23, 47, 75. Conservative politician, largely responsible for the disastrous return to the gold standard 1924, and the defeat of the General Strike 1926. Keen to have a war against Nazi Germany and/or Soviet Russia, was thought dangerous in peacetime, but was elected war leader and formed coalition government in June 1940.

Cripps, Stafford page 53. Expelled from Parliamentary Labour Party 1939 for joining Churchill in call for war. Ambassador to Moscow 1940-42. Minister of Aircraft Production in 1943.

Goering, Hermann page 71. Nazi, Field Marshall of German forces, deputy and designated successor to Hitler.

Hitler, Adolf pages 9, 47, 75. Nazi dictator of Germany. Chancellor isnce 1933. By the Enabling Act of 1934, he alone enacted all German statute law.

Laval, Pierre page 9. Nazi puppet Prime Minister of France.

Morrison, Herbert page 53. Home Secretary. Had been Conscientious Objector in 1914-18 war. Ordered that COs should not be subjected to "cat and mouse" treatment, and resisted proposals to prohibit publication of anti-war opinions.

Mussolini, Benito pages 9, 47, 75. Dictator of Italy since 1921. Sometime revolutionary socialist, had translated Kropotkin into Italian and kept Stirner's *Ego and His Own* on his office desk. Declared war as ally of Germany after Germany overran France, June 1940.

Roosevelt, Franklin D. pages 9, 47, 75. President of the USA since 1932, broke precedent by being elected for a third term in 1940. Supported allies (while promising not to "send our American boys to die in Europe"), but inhibited from declaring war by Isolationist movement, until 1941. Partly paralysed by polio, he saluted with his left hand.

Stalin, Josef pages 9, 28, 47, 75. (J. V. Djugashvilli). Had been "Dictator" of Soviet Russia, but in 1943 was an ally and therefore "Prime Minister". Crushed all opposition to his personal rule by the "purges" of the 1930s. Treaty with Hitler 1939, for conquest and division of Poland. Became ally when Germany invaded Russia in 1941.

Tojo, Hideki page 9. Chief Minister of Japan. Responsible for attack on Pearl Harbour 1941, which brought both Japan and the USA into the war.

Some political symbols, such as the **Swastika** of Nazism and the **Hammer and Sickle** and **Star** of Soviet Communism, are familiar today. Less familiar, perhaps, are the **Rising Sun** from the Japanese flag (pages 41, 49) and the **Fasces**, a bundle of sticks with an axe (pages 41, 49, 55), the symbol of Italian Fascism.

V for Victory (pages 23, 51, 55) signified confidence in allied victory, and was used as defiant graffito in countries under Nazi occupation. V in Morse code was used as the call sign for radio broadcasts to Europe. Churchill acknowledged applause by holding two fingers in a V, as on page 75.

Donald Rooum

John Olday 1905-1977. Born Arthur William Oldag. According to his autobiography *Kingdom of Rags* (1938), he took part in the German revolt which ended the 1914-18 war, as an ammunition carrier at a Spartakist machine-gun post where all but he were killed. A successful artist in the Weimar Republic, he continued as a satirical cartoonist under Nazi rule, until fleeing to Britain in 1938.

About the time war broke out he joined the Royal Pioneer Corps (the only British regiment open to German nationals), from which he deserted in 1943. From late 1944 until April 1946 he was in prison, sentenced to one year for "stealing by finding" an identity card, followed immediately by military imprisonment for desertion. In the 1950s he migrated to Australia where he worked as a cabaret artist, returning to Britain in the 1960s.

His cartoons appeared regularly in *War Commentary* from 1942 to 1944, and irregularly in *Freedom* in the late 1940s and early 1960s. Some of his *War Commentary* cartoons are reproduced in Berneri *Neither East Nor West*.

Marie Louise Berneri 1918-1949. Active in the anarchist movement in France during the 1930s, came to Britain in 1937 after her father Camillo Berneri had been killed in Spain by men wearing Communist armbands. One of the main editorial writers of *Spain and the World*, afterwards *War Commentary* then *Freedom*, she also wrote and edited pamphlets and was an outstanding organiser and public speaker.

As the war in Europe was ending, in April 1945, she and three other editors of *War Commentary* were charged with "conspiring to contravene Defence Regulation 39A", under which it was an offence to "incite members of His Majesty's Forces to disaffection". The others were found guilty and sentenced to nine months in prison, while she was acquitted on a technicality.

Freedom Press currently publishes a collection of her newspaper articles, *Neither East nor West* (with cartoons by John Olday), and her brilliant *Journey Through Utopia*, first published 1950, and in print ever since.

CONTENTS

It is probable - nay, certain that among the means which will next time be at their disposal will be agencies and processes of destruction wholesale, unlimited and perhaps, once launched, uncontrollable . . . Death stands at attention, obedient, ready to shear away the peoples en masse; ready if called on to pulverize, without hope of repair, what is left of civilization. He awaits only the word of command.

Winston Churchill, *The Aftermath.*
[quoted on the title page of the 1943 edition]

1. PROPAGANDA

I doubt if it is his appetite for birds that makes the cat with the yellow eyes feel guilty. If you were able to talk to him in his own language and formulate your accusations against him as a bird-eater, he would probably be merely puzzled and look on you as a crank. If you pursued the argument and compelled him to moralize his position, he would, I fancy, explain that the birds were very wicked creatures and that their cruelties to the worms and the insects were more than flesh and blood could stand. He would work himself up into a generous idealisation of himself as the guardian of law and order amid the bloody strife of the cabbage patch – the preserver of the balance of nature. If cats were as clever as we, they would compile an atrocities blue-book about worms.

Robert Lynd, *The Pleasures of Ignorance*

[left to right: Mussolini, Hitler, Tojo, Stalin, Churchill, Laval (above) Roosevelt.]

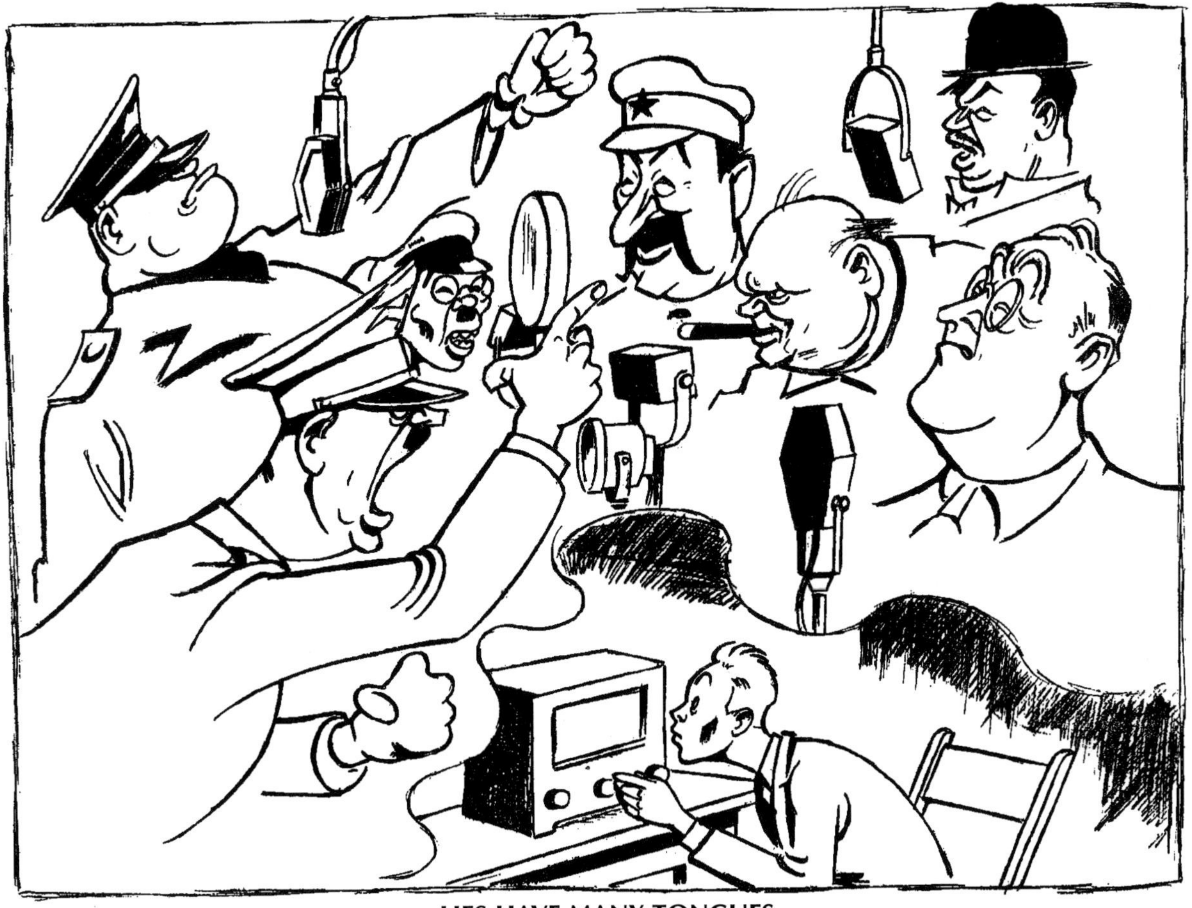

LIES HAVE MANY TONGUES

[Armament manufacturers] have been active in fomenting war scares, disseminated false reports about armament programmes of other governments, and by attempted bribery of government officials and by their control of newspapers, have played one country off against another.

League of Nations Document A81, 1921

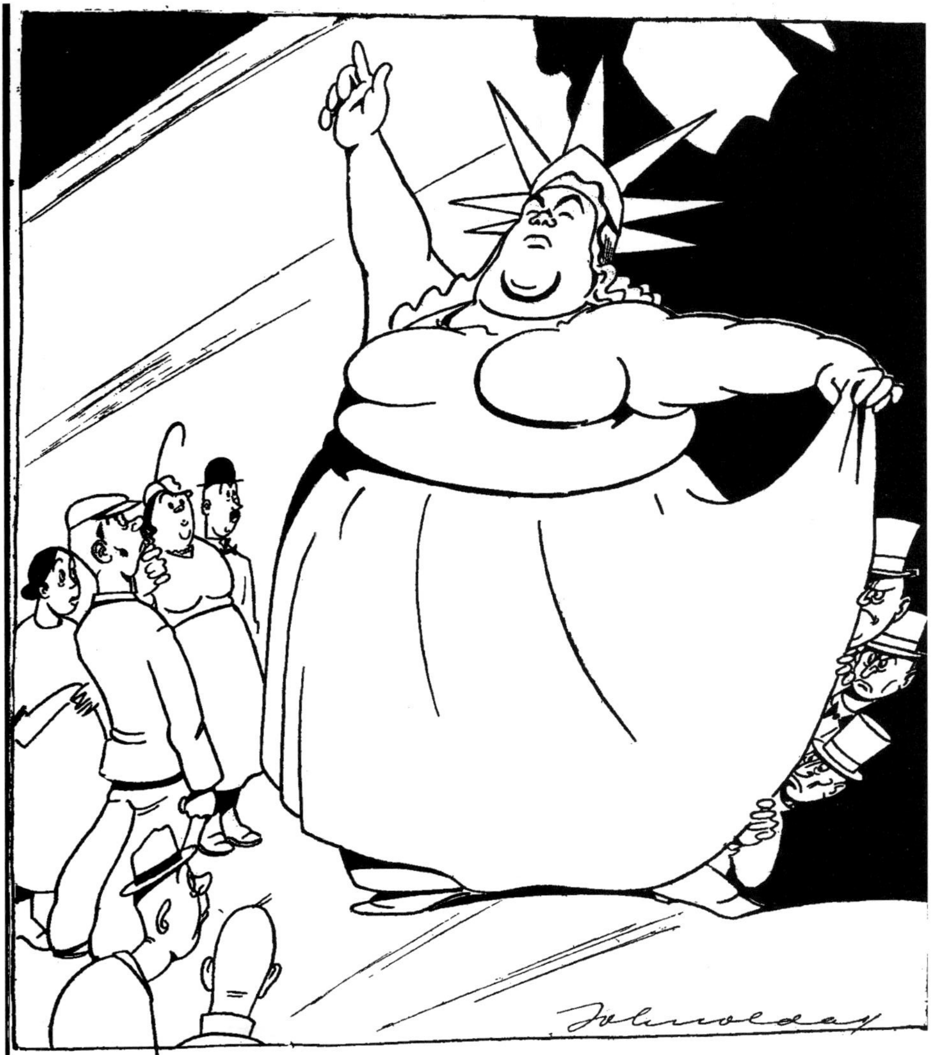

THE PRESS "I AM THE TRUTH"

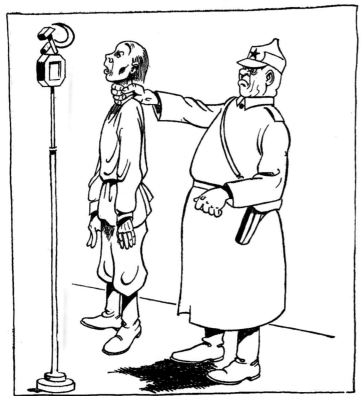

THE RUSSIAN WORKER DOES NOT COMPLAIN

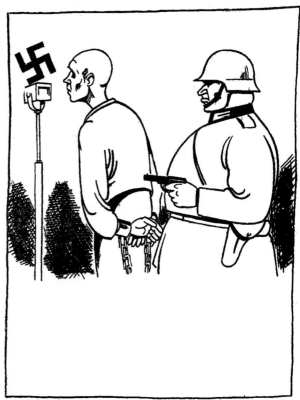

GERMANY CALLING!

THE VOICE OF FREE DEMOCRACY

13

2. THE SYSTEMS

New York Stock Exchange had a boom yesterday following Von Ribbentrop's speech at Danzig. Wall Street interprets the speech as meaning a long war. Stocks rose almost to the highest levels of the year.

Daily Sketch, 26th October 1939

The arms manufacturers over the world are the cause of most of this trouble in Europe . . .

The Nye investigations in Washington revealed the futility of League armament discussions, while British, American and French armament manufacturers were selling enormous supplies of arms to all the world and were maintaining secret agents at Geneva to defeat the very purpose of the Disarmament Conference . . .

Nor have the English been better. They have themselves violated the Versailles Treaty in selling aircraft and other war materials to Germany.

Ambassador Dodds' Diary, 1933-1938

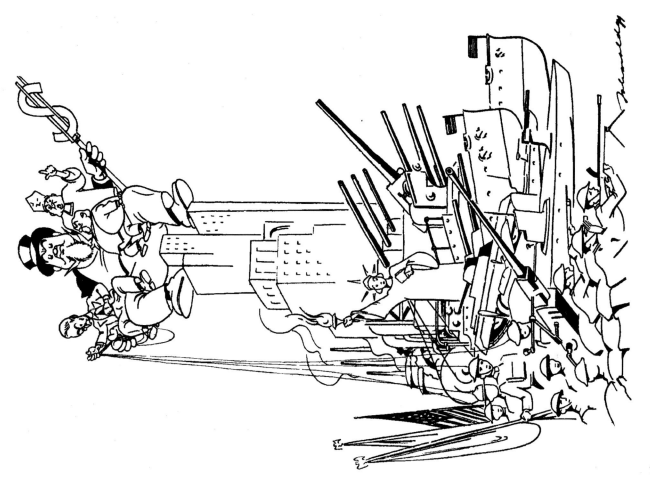

DOLLAR DEMOCRACY

15

America is still nominally on the gold standard, but as the present holding of gold would permit almost unlimited expansion of credit, the fact has no real significance. Nor is it easy to see how, in the world at large, gold can ever again play a prominent monetary role. The world outside the United States has no gold worth speaking of, and is not likely to have any means of procuring any.

Oscar Hobson, *News Chronicle*, 17th June 1942

It has puzzled many people for some time why at this stage of the war great quantities of gold should be blasted out of the Transvaal rock, refined, and shipped to the United States only to be interred in the underground vaults of Fort Knox, Kentucky. More than 300,000 native labourers are employed in the mines alone; explosives, transport, and shipping space are used in this apparently futile traffic. But so long as the United States Government demanded gold in part payment for goods supplied to the sterling area the gold had to be raised and sent.

Financial Editor, *Manchester Guardian*, 6th February 1942

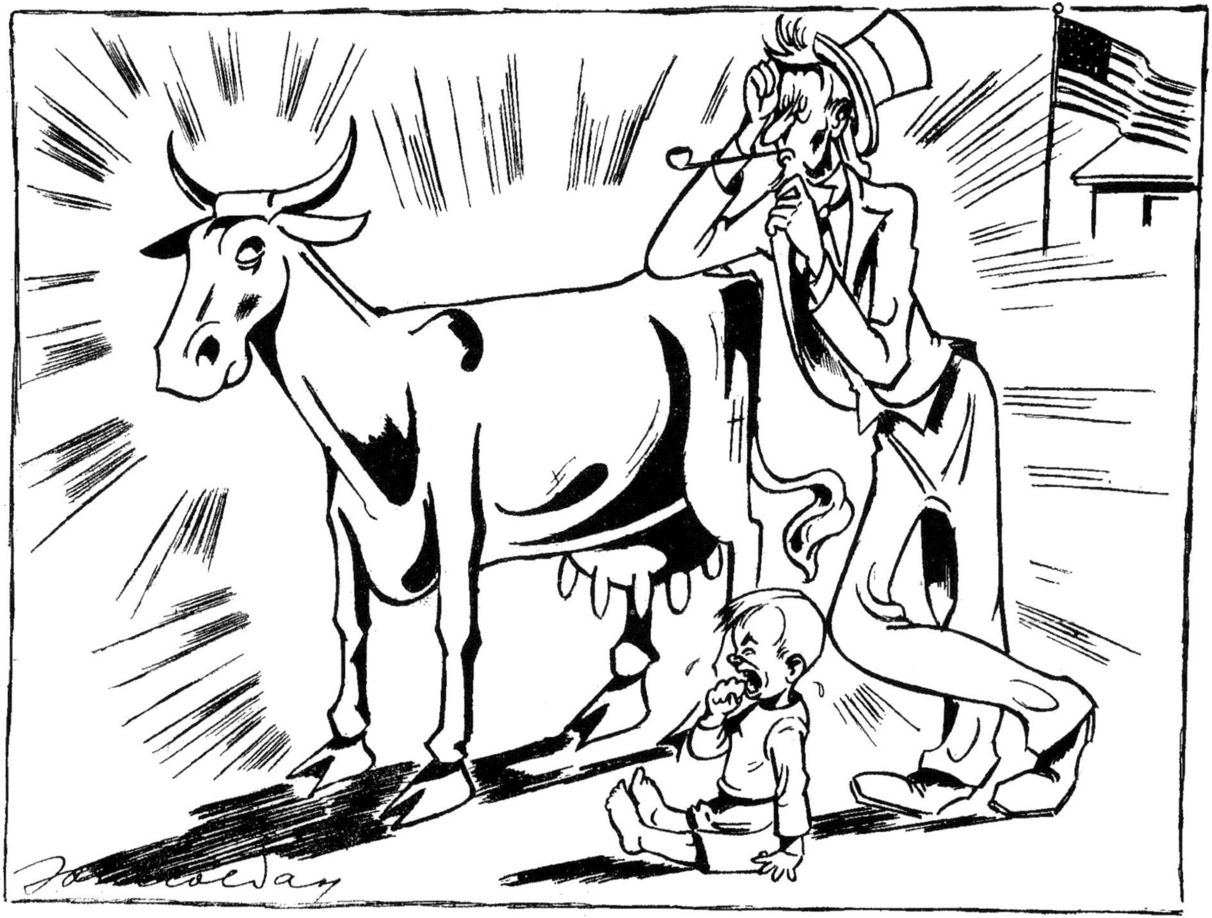

I CAN'T EAT GOLD!

Willie Vinson, 25-year-old Negro, was dragged from his hospital bed and lynched on July 13th. Before being hanged from a cottage gin winch outside Texarkana, Vinson was tied to an automobile and dragged through the streets. He already had a bullet wound in the stomach received when the mob attacked him in a cafe where he worked as a dishwasher. He was shot when he tried to defend himself with a knife.

Industrial Worker, 25th July 1942

A mob of over 300 to-day seized and critically injured a 30-year-old negro held in the city gaol at Sikeston, Missouri, on a charge of having criminally attacked a white woman. The crowd then dragged the victim, Cleo Wright, through the negro quarter of the town, soaked his body in petrol and burned it.

Evening Standard 26th January 1942

[This drawing should be understood in the light of knowledge available to the authors in 1943. Please see the Introduction page 3.]

I THANK GOD I AM NOT A WICKED JEW BAITER!

From September, 1938 – February, 1939, Germany imported 39,000 tons of pig iron from Britain. The normal importation is 5,000 tons!

In the first months of 1939 Britain exported to Germany 5,136 tons of brass and alloys of copper and 1,156 tons of aluminium and its alloys.

However, we will get it all back in some form or another!
Oliver Brown, *The Hypocrisy and Folly of this War*

The charge that Britain did want war shows strange forgetfulness of the help given by the Governments of Lord Baldwin and Mr. MacDonald to the early progress of the Nazi regime.
The London Times, 26th October 1939

THE NAZI BABY LACKS NOTHING

We assure Winston Churchill that we stand behind him as a movement to a man and to a woman. Never has a Prime Minister had a more loyal Party to follow him than has Winston Churchill in the Labour Party.

W. H. Green, Chairman of the Labour Party, June 1942

I myself would like to see the Prime Minister given more power. No democracy can ever wage a war. In war-time you want an autocracy or what is commonly called a dictator and although we are not ready yet for a dictator, and perhaps will not be until something terrible happens, still I would like to see greater powers given to the Prime Minister.

Lord Clanwilliam in a speech reported by the *Manchester Guardian*, 27th July 1942

[Churchill]

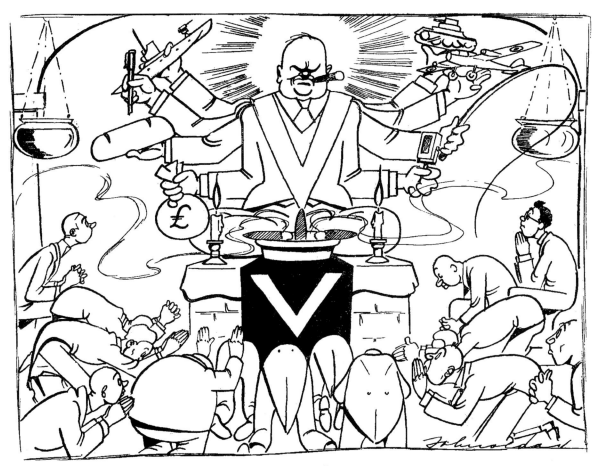

"DEMOCRATIC" LEADER

23

The capitalists are in your [the workers'] hands. Refuse to make munitions, refuse to make armaments, and they are helpless. They would have to hand the control of the country over to you.
Stafford Cripps quoted in the *Evening Citizen*

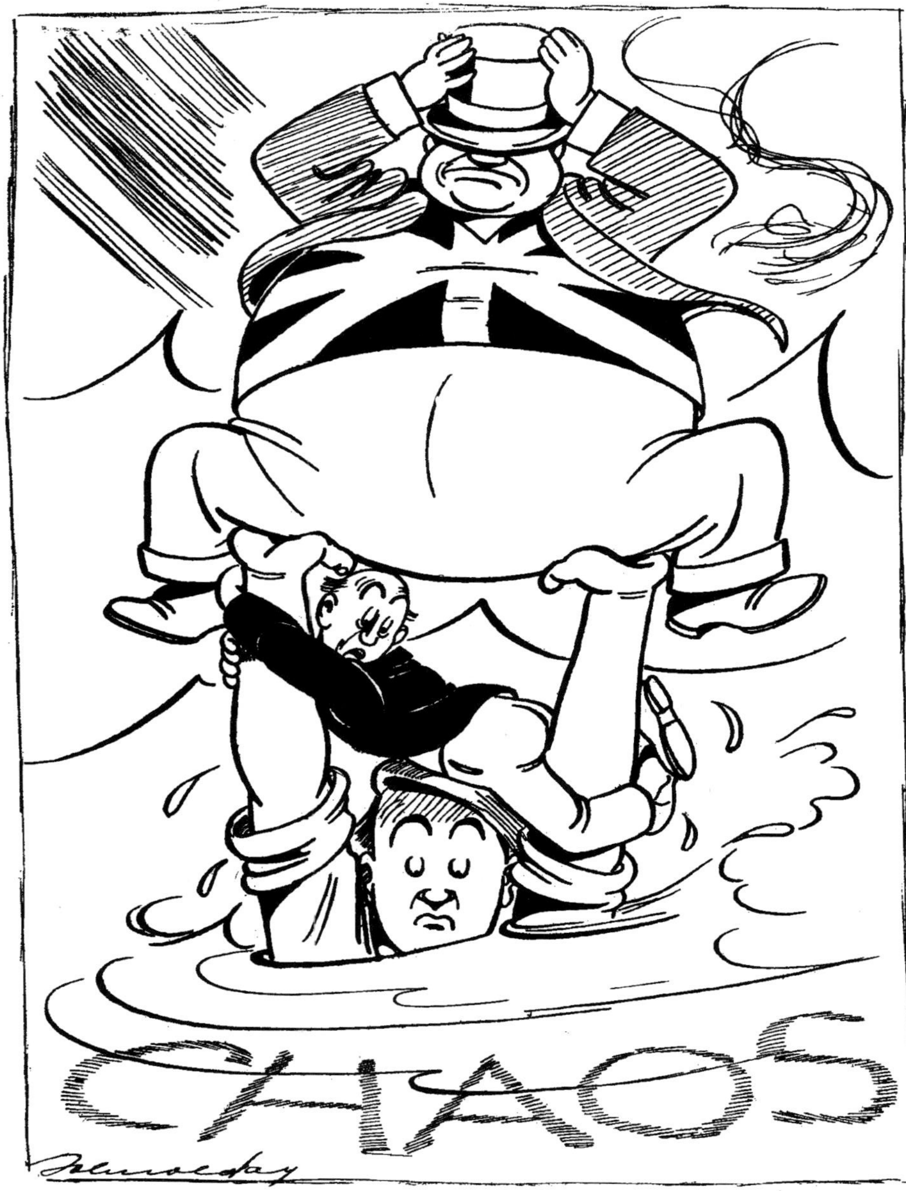
CHAOS

WILL HE SEE ME THROUGH?

In the Soviet Union, in the land where the dictatorship of the proletariat is in force, no important political or organizational problem is ever decided by our soviets and other mass organizations, without directives from our party. In this sense, we may say that the dictatorship of the proletariat is substantially the dictatorship of the party, as the force which most effectively guides the proletariat.

J. Stalin, *Leninism*, Vol. 1, 1928

Nine hundred and nine controllers control the nation's wool. Five hundred and eighty-three controllers control the nation's timber. Between two and three thousand controllers control the nation's food. Sixty-eight dictate to the paper industry. Sixty-four settle the aluminium business. Fifty-four look after leather. Fifty-four others have become little Hitlers in hemp. There are thirty jute Goerings and fifty-one cotton Commissars. The Select Committee on Expenditure may discover that each and all of these are indispensable. But we recall that Pizarro set out to conquer Peru with only thirteen companions, while Horatio held the bridge with a couple of office boys.

Evening Standard, 25th January 1940

RUSSIAN WORKER TO BRITISH WORKER:
"DON'T YOU SEE WHAT YOU ARE MISSING COMRADE?"

27

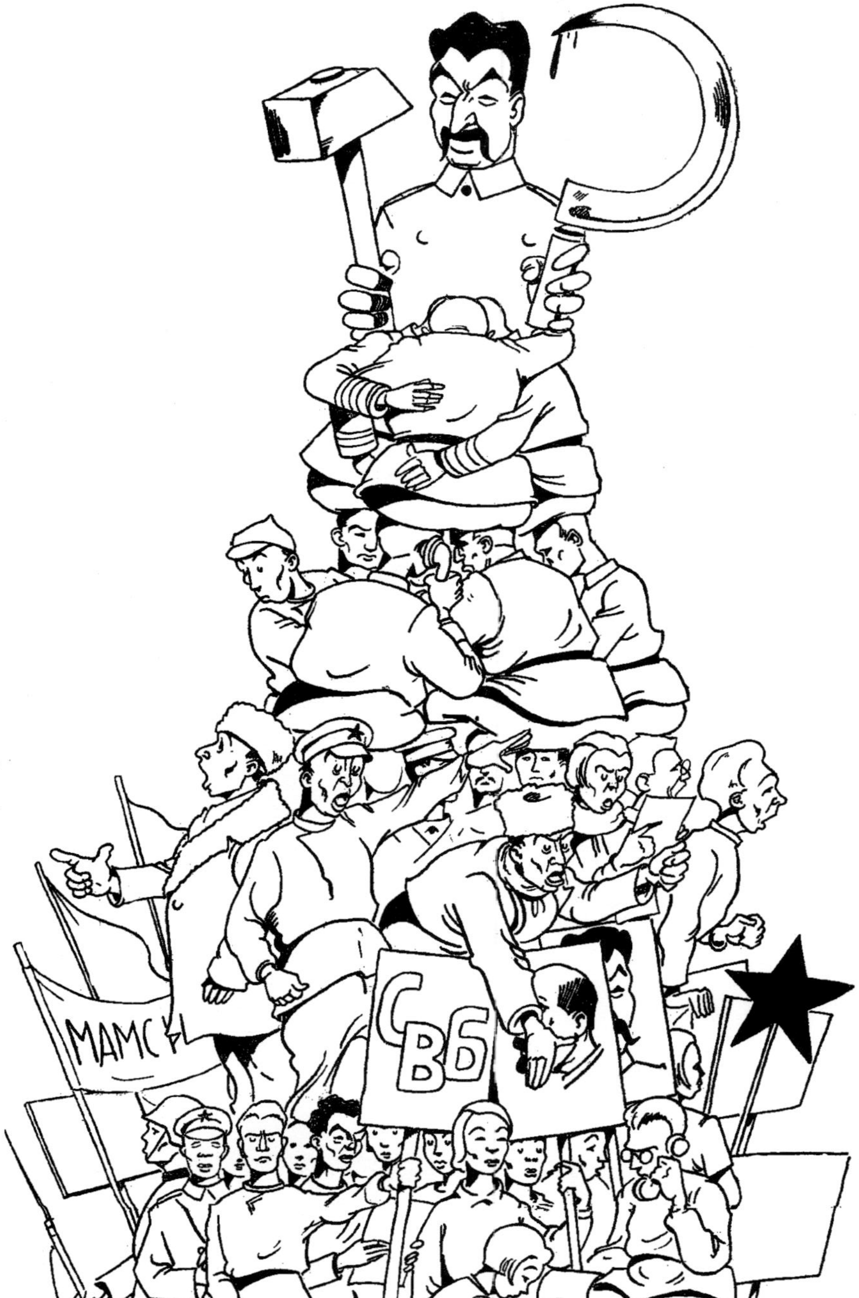
МАМС
СВБ

THE WORKERS' PARADISE

There are at the head of the party three or four thousand leaders; they are our superior officers. Then come from thirty to forty thousand members occupying medium posts: this is the body of our subaltern officers. At last, from a hundred to a hundred and fifty thousand form the body of our sub-officers.

Stalin in a speech at the Plenum of the Central Committee of the Party in March 1937

Admittedly there is in the U.S.S.R. of to-day no sign of the coming of identical, or even of substantially equal incomes for all workers by hand or by brain. On the contrary, the utmost use continues to be made of such forms of remuneration as piecework rates and payment according to social value (i.e., scarcity) or technical skill, not to mention also such devices for intensification of effort as socialist competition and Stakhanovite rationalism of industrial technique – all candidly justified by their demonstrated results in increasing production.

. . . The effect of those devices is to make the maximum divergence of individual incomes in the U.S.S.R., taking the extreme instances, probably as great as the corresponding divergence in income paid for actual participation in work, in Great Britain if not in the United States.

Sidney and Beatrice Webb, *Soviet Communism*

3. THE STRUGGLE FOR FREEDOM

Those who go to war against a people in order to stop their progress toward liberty and to destroy the rights of man, must be condemned by all and be considered not just as enemies, but as assassins and brigands.

Robespierre

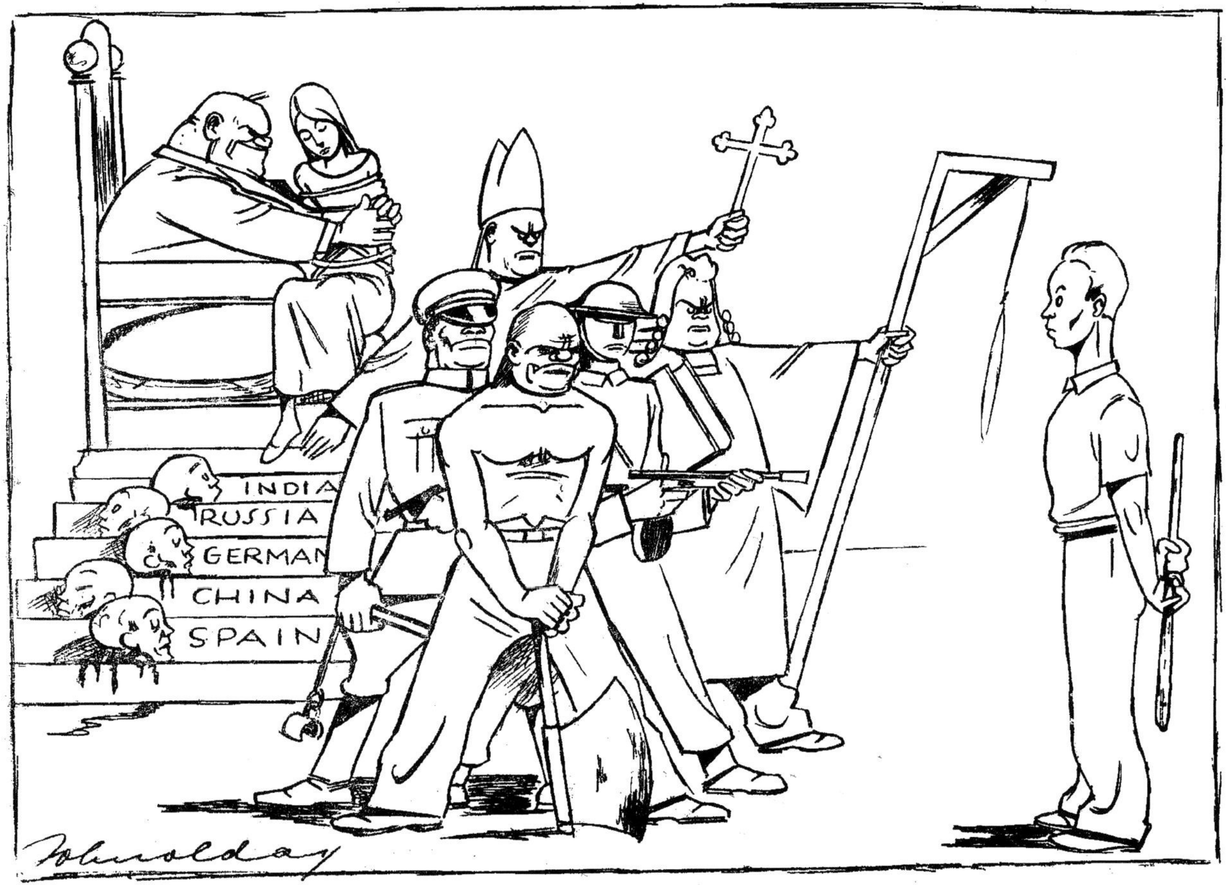
INDIA
RUSSIA
GERMAN
CHINA
SPAIN

COME AND GET IT

Never was there a nation so noble as ours, so splendid in its public and private integrity with such widespread ideals of progress or such general devotion to betterment.

Sometimes you hear ancient Greece cracked up to you. Bear in mind that in fair Athens at the height of her fame there were 19 slaves for every free citizen who had a vote.

That is not the democracy that we are aiming at, but there never yet was a great nation that did not have at least a subsection on a level that was in fact or figure slavery.

William Barkley in the *Daily Express*, 17th March 1942

WHY DON'T YOU SHAKE THEM OFF?

33

J. H. Thomas, representing the railwaymen, found early in the Strike, that his duties took him to Buckingham Palace. King George asked him a number of questions, and expressed his sympathy for the miners. At the end of the talk, His Majesty, who was gravely disturbed, remarked, it is said: 'Well, Thomas, if the worst happens, I suppose all this – ' (with a gesture indicating his surroundings) ' – will vanish?'

Fortunately for Britain and the world, it did not come to the worst. The Trades Unions saw to that.

J. R. Clynes, *Memoirs*

It must not be forgotten that apart from the rights and wrongs of the calling of a General Strike, there would in any case, with the miners' lockout, have been widespread unofficial fighting in all parts of the country, which would have produced anarchy in the movement.

Ernest Bevin in *The Record*

What I dreaded about this strike more than anything else was this: if by any chance it should have got out of the hands of those who would be able to exercise some control, every sane man knows what would have happened. I thank God it never did.

J. H. Thomas in the House of Commons, 13th May 1926

DON'T KILL HIM FOR GOD'S SAKE!

The English workers follow supinely a Conservative government's policy of pro-Fascist intervention in Spain. The French workers pride themselves in their blind discipline to the "Front Populaire" which is governing France to the best interests of the "two hundred families" who would rather see the monarchy restored both in France and in Spain than lose their Spanish dividends. And as for Russia, Mr. Litvinoff put its position in a nutshell when he said in Geneva: "We have sacrificed Spain" . . . rather than compromise our friendship with semi-feudal England and our alliance with plutocratic France.

Max Sartin, *Spain and the World,* December 1937

THE SPANISH REVOLUTION FAILED

37

4. WHOSE WAR?

We must ascertain what are the contributing factors to the present world situation, and it will be found that possibly the biggest contributor is this country, is not Germany, for one of the most potent causes of world disorder has been our dominant financial policy.

Ernest Bevin at Southport Labour Conference, 1939

Any attempt to interpret literally the phrase "equality of sacrifice" would of course not help prosecute the war to victory, but would hopelessly sabotage it. There is not, and cannot be, any literal equality of sacrifice as between workers and capitalists in this war. The workers must make the main sacrifices, and they have enough common sense to know, and enough patriotism not to object to it.

Earl Browder in his book, Victory and After

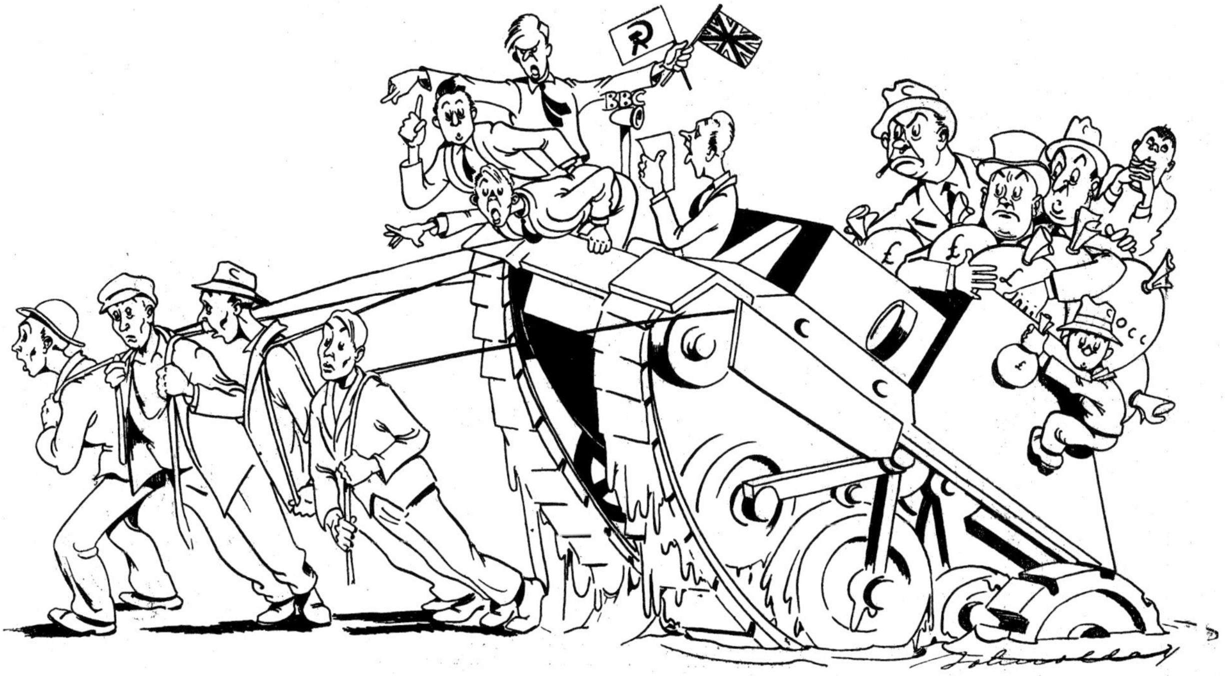
BBC

BEFORE THE WAR: SORRY HE CAN'T HELP YOU

WHEN WAR STARTS: HELP! HELP!

The British Government is a traitor to democracy and to the interests of its own country. It prefers to drift on without an intelligible foreign policy, engage in competitive national rearmament, fatalistically moving towards an imperialist war of the old order. Then I suppose we shall be expected to support it.

Herbert Morrison, Minister of Supply, 1940

My hatred of Fascism had developed by five years' intensive anti-Fascist propaganda, which led to a position where I did not see in time the true role of British imperialism, and saw only German Fascism as the main enemy of the British working-class movement.

Harry Pollitt, *Daily Worker*, 23rd November 1939

Kill the Hun and the Italian in their own country and not in someone else's. It makes a tremendous difference where they are killed.

Lord Trenchard, at a Unilever "bomber" luncheon, *Daily Herald*, 21st November 1940

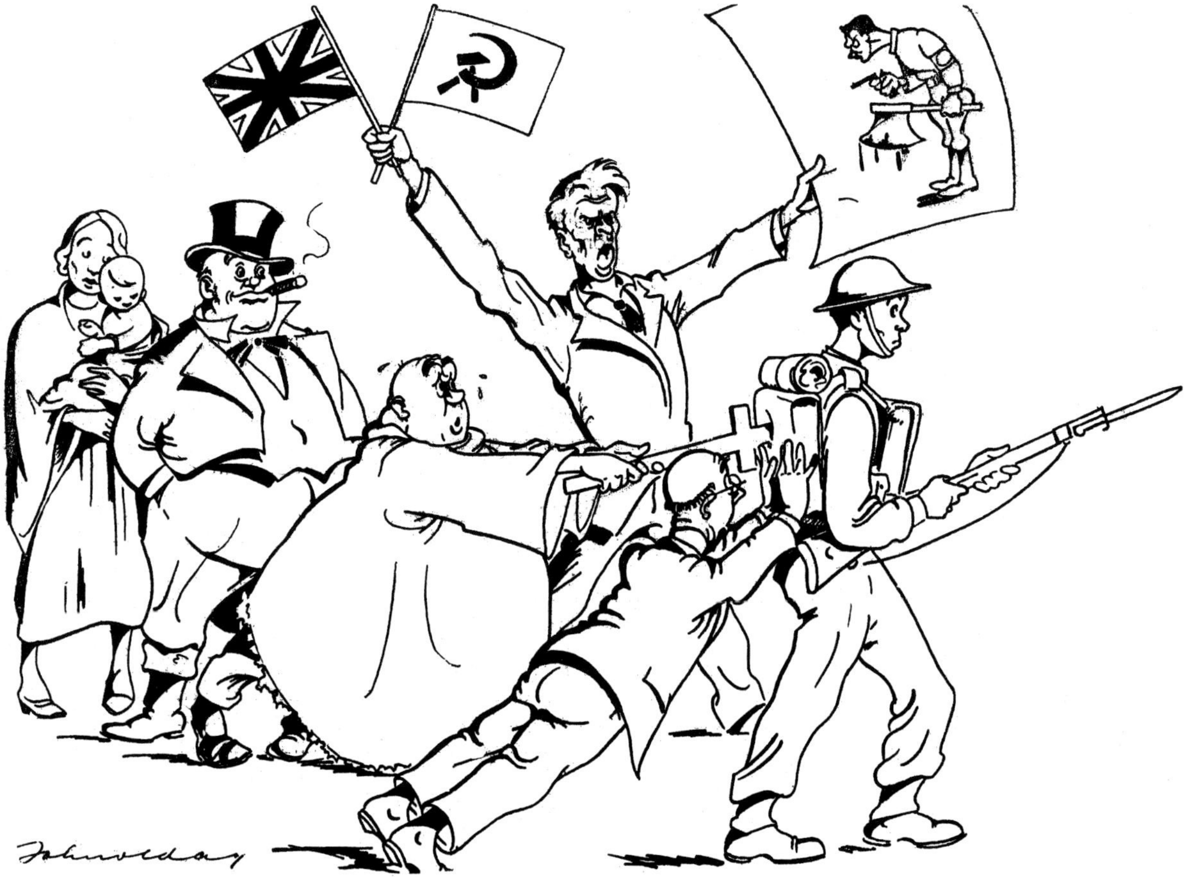

DEFEND OUR HERITAGE

In history the name of God is the terrible club with which all divinely inspired men, the great "virtuous geniuses", have beaten down liberty, dignity, reason, and prosperity of man.

Michael Bakunin

May God help us in the great ordeal which now awaits us.

Archbishop of Canterbury and other dignitaries of the Church

When you come to think of it, it is a great honour to be chosen by God to be his ally in so great a contest.

Canon C. Morgan Smith

We thank God that He gave us a speedy victory to our arms . . . We thank him that injustice, centuries old, has been broken down through His grace . . .

The German Evangelical "Opposition" in the Spiritual Councils
Proclamation on the capture of Poland

If there be a God, then what He would like me to do is to paint as much of the map of Africa British-red as possible. The government of the world by its finest race is the aim I have in view.

Cecil Rhodes's last will and testament

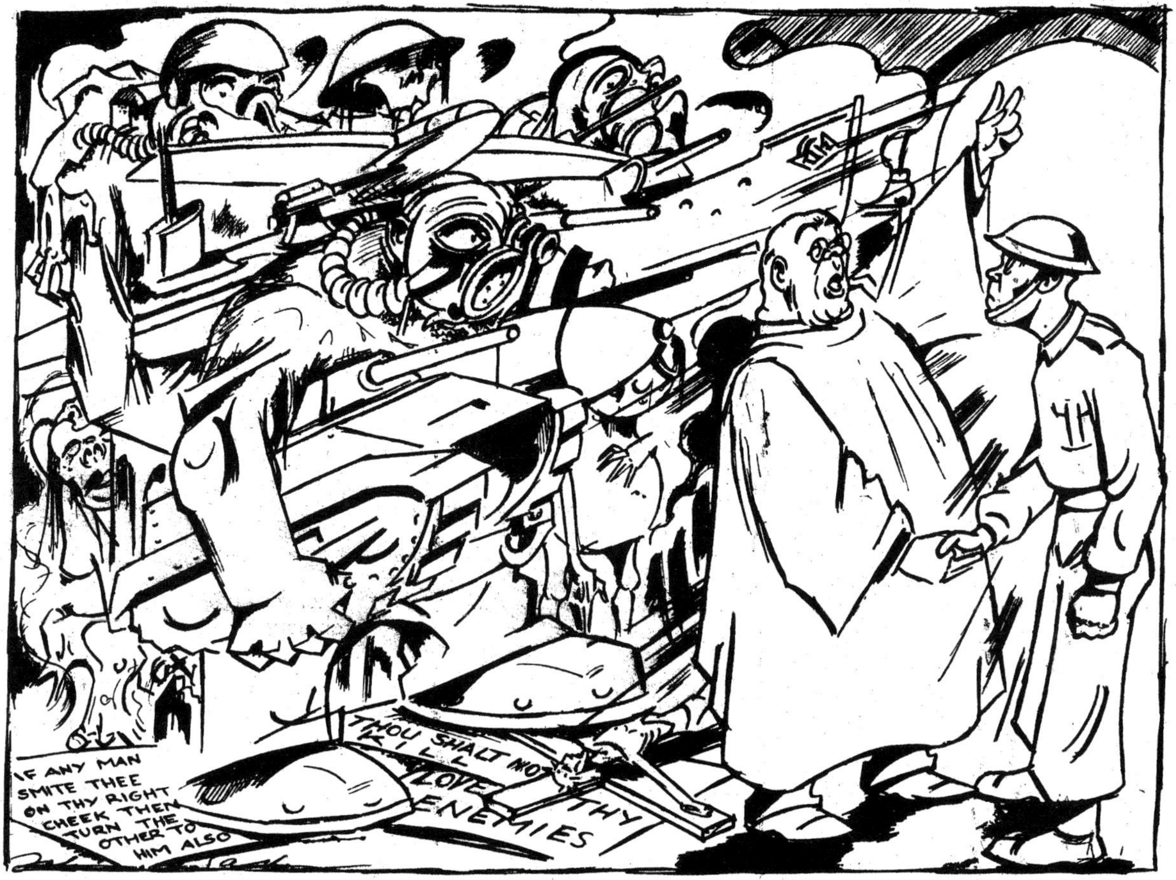
IF ANY MAN SMITE THEE ON THY RIGHT CHEEK THEN TURN THE OTHER TO HIM ALSO
THOU SHALT NOT KILL
LOVE THY ENEMIES

GOD IS ON OUR SIDE

I confess I see no reason whatever why, either in act, or in word, or in sympathy, we should go individually, or internationally against Japan in this matter. Japan has got a very powerful case based on fundamental realities . . . when you look at the fact that Japan needs markets and that it is imperative for her, in the world in which she lives, that there should be some sort of peace and order, then who is there among us to cast the first stone and to say that Japan ought not to have acted with the object of creating peace and order in Manchuria and defending herself against the continual aggression of vigorous Chinese nationalism? Our whole policy in India, our whole policy in Egypt, stand condemned if we condemn Japan.

L. S. Amery, now Minister for India, 7th February 1933

[left to right: Roosevelt, Churchill, Stalin, Hitler, Mussolini; the Japanese is not a particular individual]

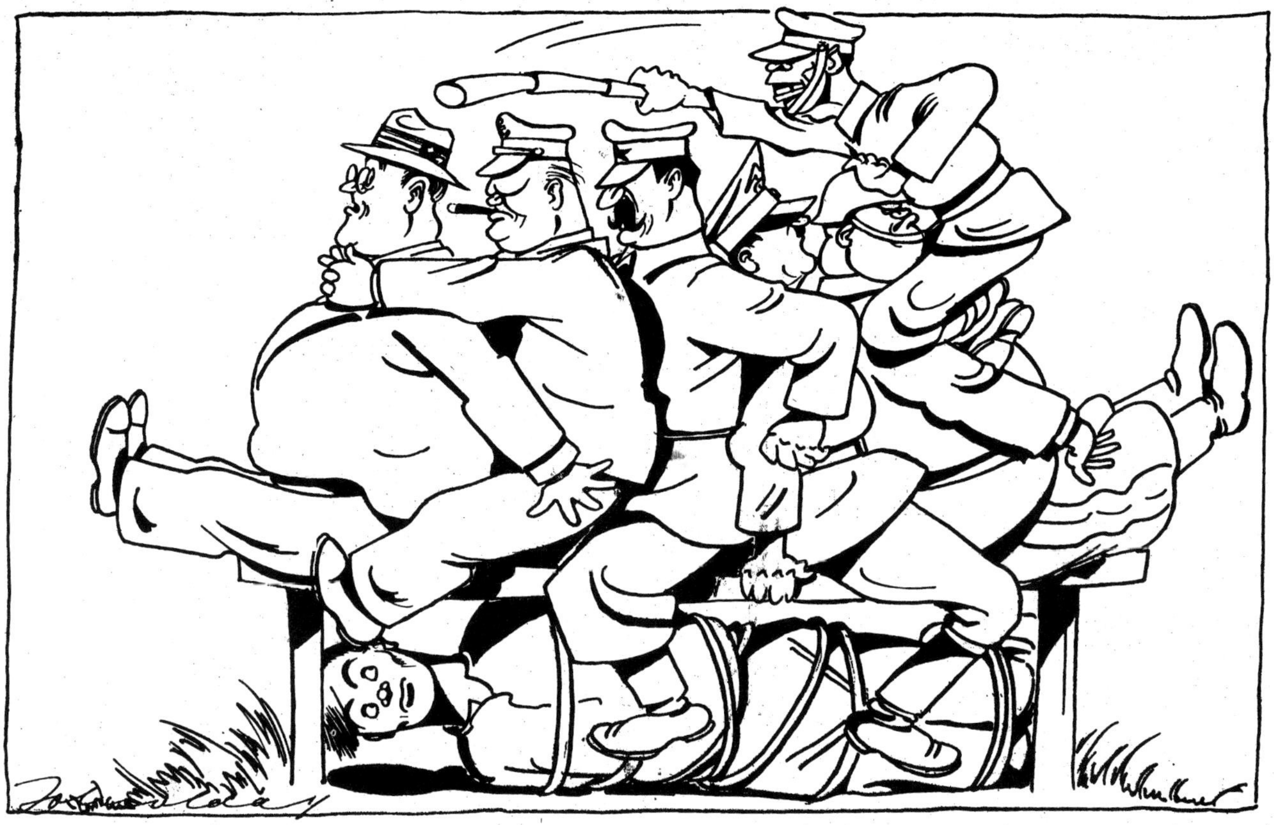

WHO WILL COME OUT ON TOP?

5. WHAT ARE WE FIGHTING FOR?

The Anglo-Saxon race is infallibly destined to be the predominant race in the history and civilisation of the world.

Mr. Joseph Chamberlain

We should never forget that our Empire was won by the sword, that it has been preserved safe by the sword through generations, and in the last resort in the future it could only be safeguarded by the sword.

Field-Marshal Viscount Gort, V.C., 27th July 1939

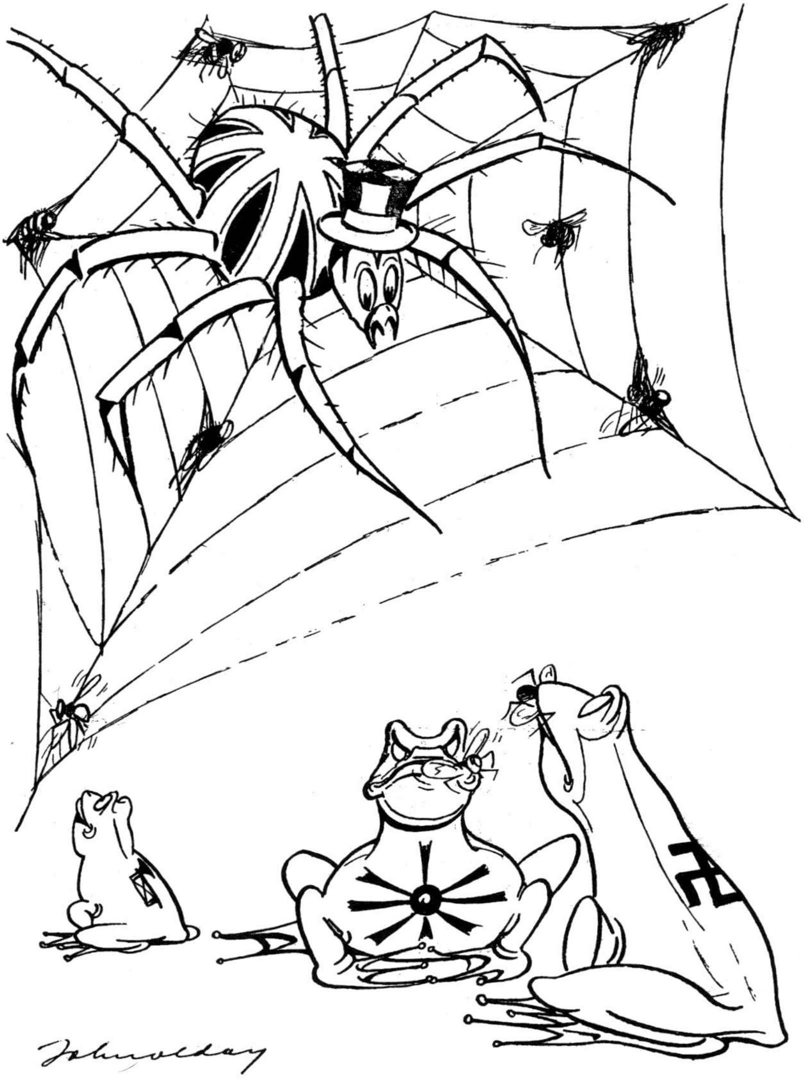
Johnolday

WHAT WE HAVE WE HOLD

[Britain and America] respect the right of all people to choose the form of government under which they will live, and they wish to see sovereign rights and self-government restored to those who have been forcibly deprived of them.

Atlantic Charter

We have no intention of casting away that most truly bright and precious jewel in the crown of the king, which more than all our other Dominions and Dependencies constitutes the glory and strength of the British Empire.

Winston Churchill, on India, 12th December 1930

THE DEFENDER OF OPPRESSED PEOPLE

Anybody who sits in the House of Commons and watches the legislation which is made to the alarm of everyone on the opposite side of the National Government, knows perfectly well that there would be no difficulty for those who form our National Government to-day to form a Fascist Government to-morrow.

Stafford Cripps quoted in the *Evening Citizen*, 15th March 1937

It is quite idle to imagine that we can combine with an imperialist Government and carry out a policy of anti-imperialism . . . Inevitably the Labour Movement, once it has assented to the policy of rearmament, will be drawn in to share the responsibilities, and, as in 1914, the Opposition will cease and our movement will become officially part of the totalitarian War Cabinet . . . The next war will mean the end of civilisation.

Stafford Cripps quoted in the *Evening Citizen*,
29th September 1936

[with black coat and tie: Bevin; with Eton collar: Beaverbrook; small figures, left to right: Attlee, Morrison, Cripps.]

LIBERTY: WILL IT STRANGLE ME?

Suppose you attained your object and Great Britain won another imperial victory, what then? British Fascism would be less brutal than German, but the world situation would be no better. Another Versailles peace, another period of acute suffering for the workers and then the next war. That is all.

Stafford Cripps in *Forward*, 3rd October 1936

[The letter V was an officially encouraged symbol of confidence in allied victory. Please see the Introduction page 5].

THAT WON'T HELP US EITHER!

Disarmament following the war would seem unlikely, and with an excellent goodwill established with a number of foreign powers, with the Admiralty, and with individual owners of speed boats, the outlook is promising.

From the chairman's speech at the annual general meeting of
Vospers, *Evening Standard*, 25th January 1940

A trade war will follow the present war

Mr. Shepard Morgan Chase, National Bank of New York,
Glasgow Citizen, 3rd January 1941

The victory of Japan clearly spells the extirpation of all European and American interest in the Far East. The victory of China, if aided by the great democracies might win for them a century of fertile and beneficent trade.

Winston Churchill, New York *Herald Tribune*,
14th August 1939

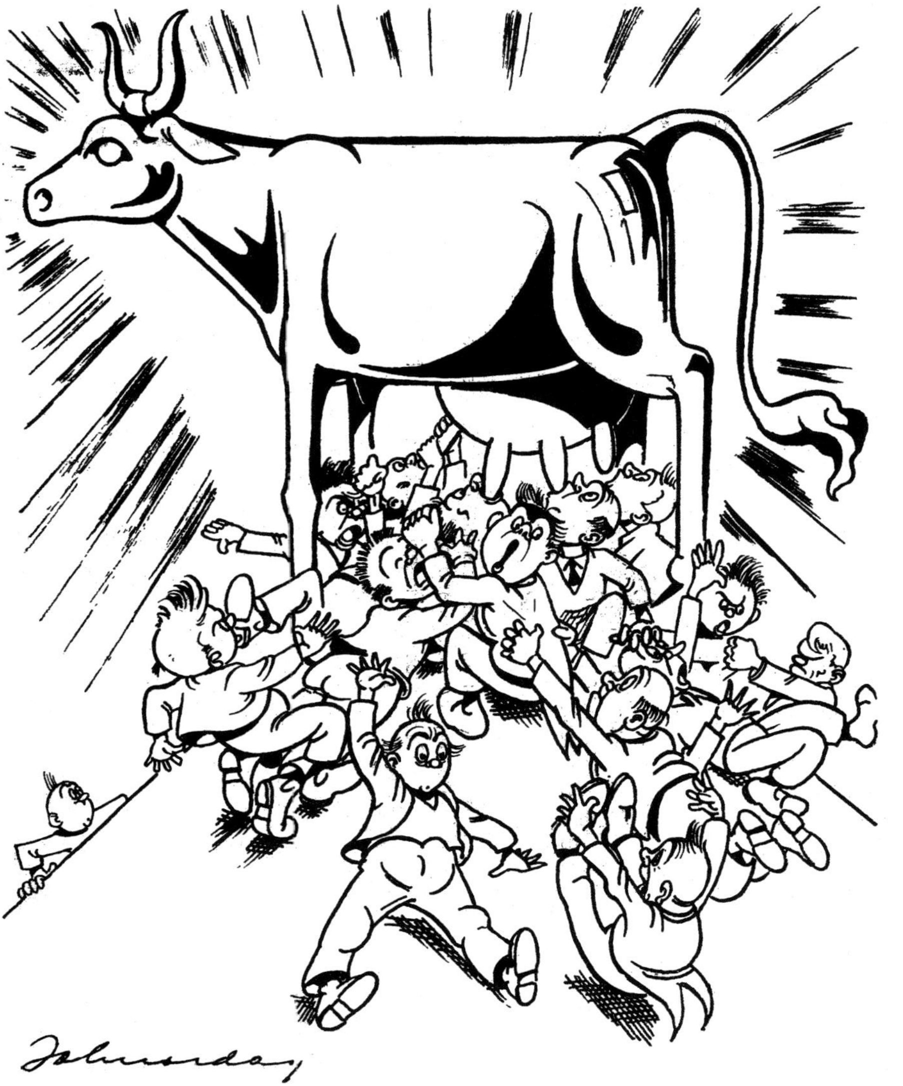

GOLD FOR THE GREEDY

I am anxious to prevent this [the Labour] movement fighting for the preservation of the Paris Bourse, the London Stock Exchange, and Wall Street.

Ernest Bevin at the 1939 Conference of the Labour Party

This war is, in one of its minor objectives, a war to make the world safe for the gold standard.

Oscar Hobson, Financial Editor of the *News Chronicle*

WE WILL LOOK AFTER LIBERTY

The swarms of cringers, dough-faces, lice of politics, planners of sly innovations for their own preferment.

Walt Whitman, *Leaves of Grass*

A CIVILIZATION WORTH FIGHTING FOR

[Amritsar, 1919] – Heaps of bodies lay here – some on their backs and some with their faces upturned. A number of them were poor innocent children. I shall never forget the sight. I saw heaps of dead bodies and I began to search for my husband. After passing through the heaps I found the dead body of my husband. The way towards it was full of blood and dead bodies.

Madam Ratan Devi in her report to Congress

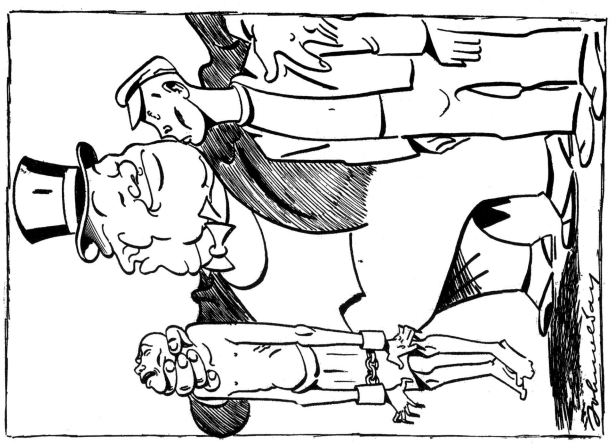

THIS WON'T HAPPEN TO YOU!

6. PEOPLE AT WAR

Advice to workers: Work like beavers and save like hell.
                    Admiral Sir William James, C-in-C Portsmouth

Nearco was invincible on the racecourse winning all the 14 races
in which he started. He earns 16,000 guineas a year in stud fees,
at 400 guineas a time. He is well insured, but Mr. Benson
decided that the loss of such a horse would be serious for English
thoroughbred breeding. So at a cost of more than £500 an air-
conditioned underground shelter was built. Every night Nearco
walks from his box to the shelter, every morning he is brought up
again.
                                    Evening Standard, 10th April 1942

I happened to remark to one of these sporting gentry that it must
be a problem to provide food for so many dogs, to which he
replied it was certainly more difficult than before the war,
particularly so with brandy, which together with the whites of
eggs forms a most suitable diet for dogs in training. Without
blushing he gave me an approximate canine menu for the day.
This included the gravy from stewed beef steak, Benger's Food,
tinned Chickens' breasts, and new laid eggs whisked with port
wine. All this to say nothing of the hares which are sacrificed.
                                New Statesman & Nation, 7th March 1942

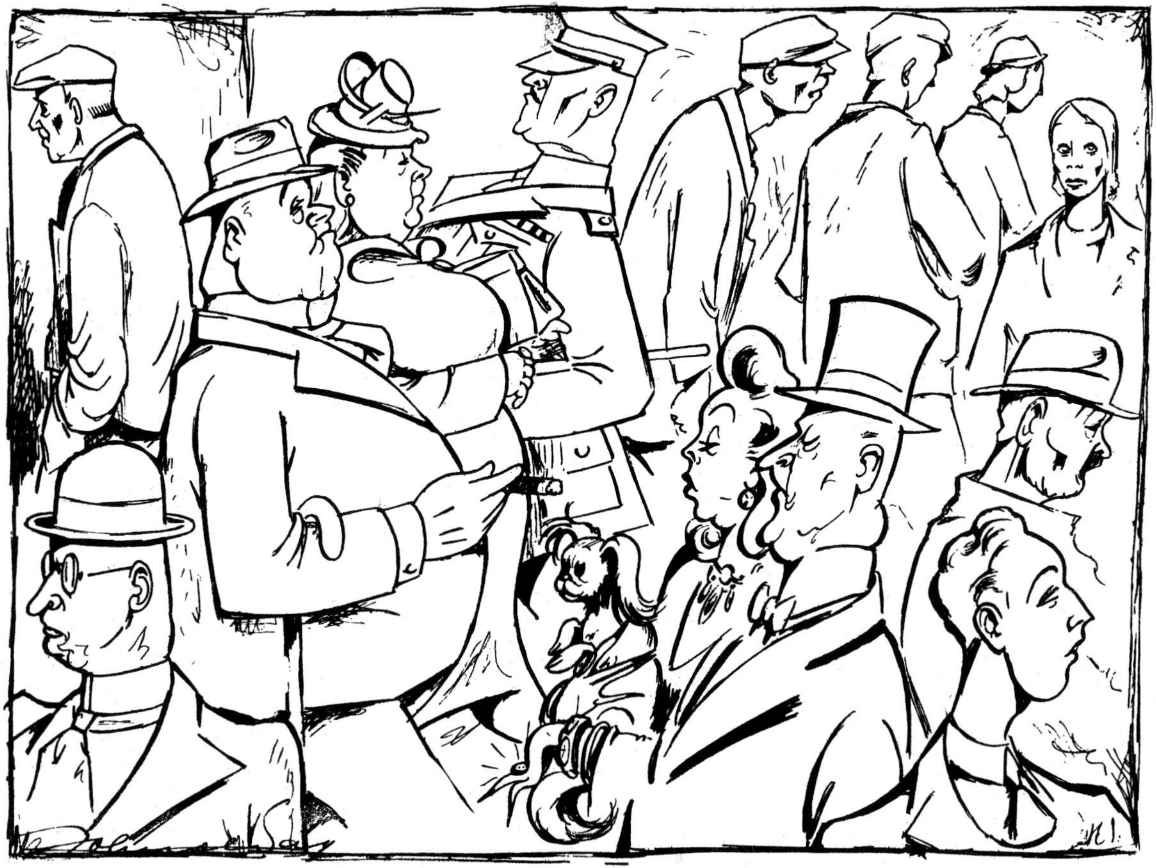

WAR WORKERS

When this idiotic shapeless war gives way to some equally idiotic and planless peace we shall be confronted by a problem of young people without prospects, untrained for anything but fighting – asking us: "And what will you do with us now?"

H. G. Wells at British Association Meeting, December 1941

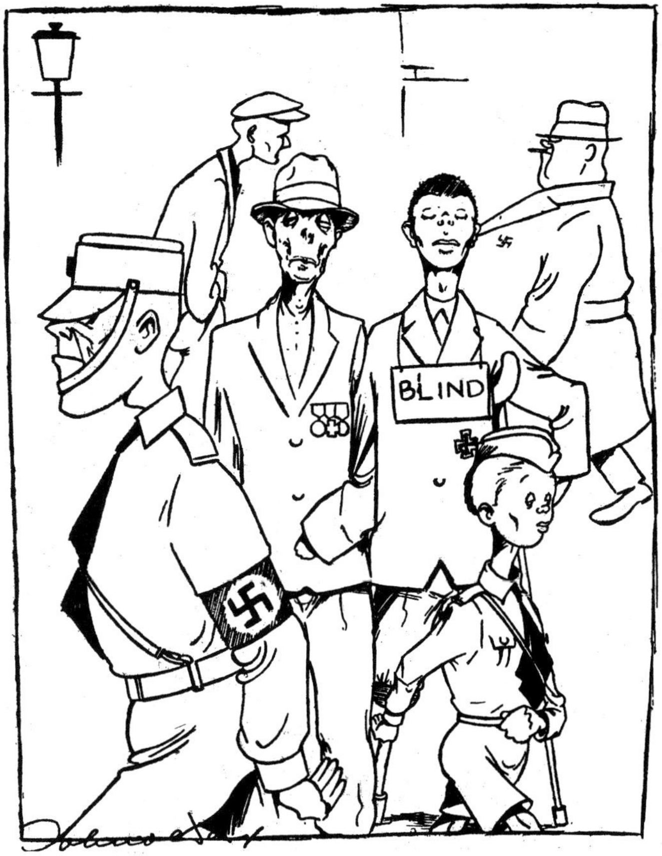
BLIND

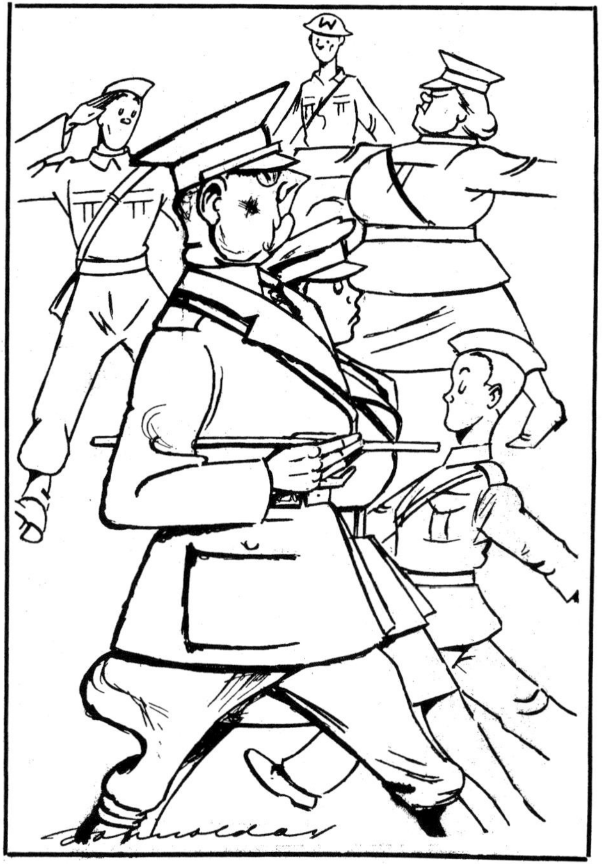

PEOPLE IN UNIFORM

YOU OUGHT TO BE IN THE ARMY

ARMISTICE DAY (194?): OCCUPATION UNCHANGED

7. POST WAR WORLD

The pages [the history of the War on the Eastern Front in 1914-1918] record the toils, perils, sufferings and passion of millions of men. Their sweat, their tears, their blood bedewed the endless plain. Ten million homes awaited the return of the warriors; a hundred cities prepared to acclaim their triumphs. But all were defeated; all were stricken; everything they had given was given in vain. The hideous injuries they inflicted and bore, the privations they endured, the grand loyalties they exemplified, all were in vain. Nothing was gained by any. They floundered in the mud, they perished in the snowdrifts, they starved in the frost. Those that survived, the veterans of countless battle days, returned, whether with the laurels of victory or the tidings of disaster, to homes already engulfed in catastrophe.

Winston Churchill, *The World Crisis, Eastern Front*

[Goering]

THEY FOUGHT FOR THE FATHERLAND

Mr. Kershner, who has been working for the American Friends'
Service Committee as Director of Relief in Europe . . . described
to me what is perhaps the most ghastly thing in war – the
unbearable tragedy of growing children who lose weight every
week, who develop tuberculosis and rickets, who faint with
hunger at school, whose legs become sticks and whose bellies
swell into drums.

New Statesman and Nation, 6th February 1943

BUILDING A HEALTHY RACE

8. THE PROCESSION OF THE VICTIMS

More people are dying in Europe and there is a sharp increase in infant mortality, according to the statistical year-book of the League of Nations. The death-rate figures do not include the war dead.

Examples of the increase in infant mortality in 1940 are Belgium 73 per 1,000 to 89, France 63 per 1,000 to 91, Italy 96 per 1,000 to 104. The general death rate in Germany per 1,000 of population increased from 11.6 in 1938 to 12.7 in 1940.

Manchester Guardian, 9th March 1942

[left to right: Mussolini, Hitler, Churchill, Stalin, Roosevelt.]

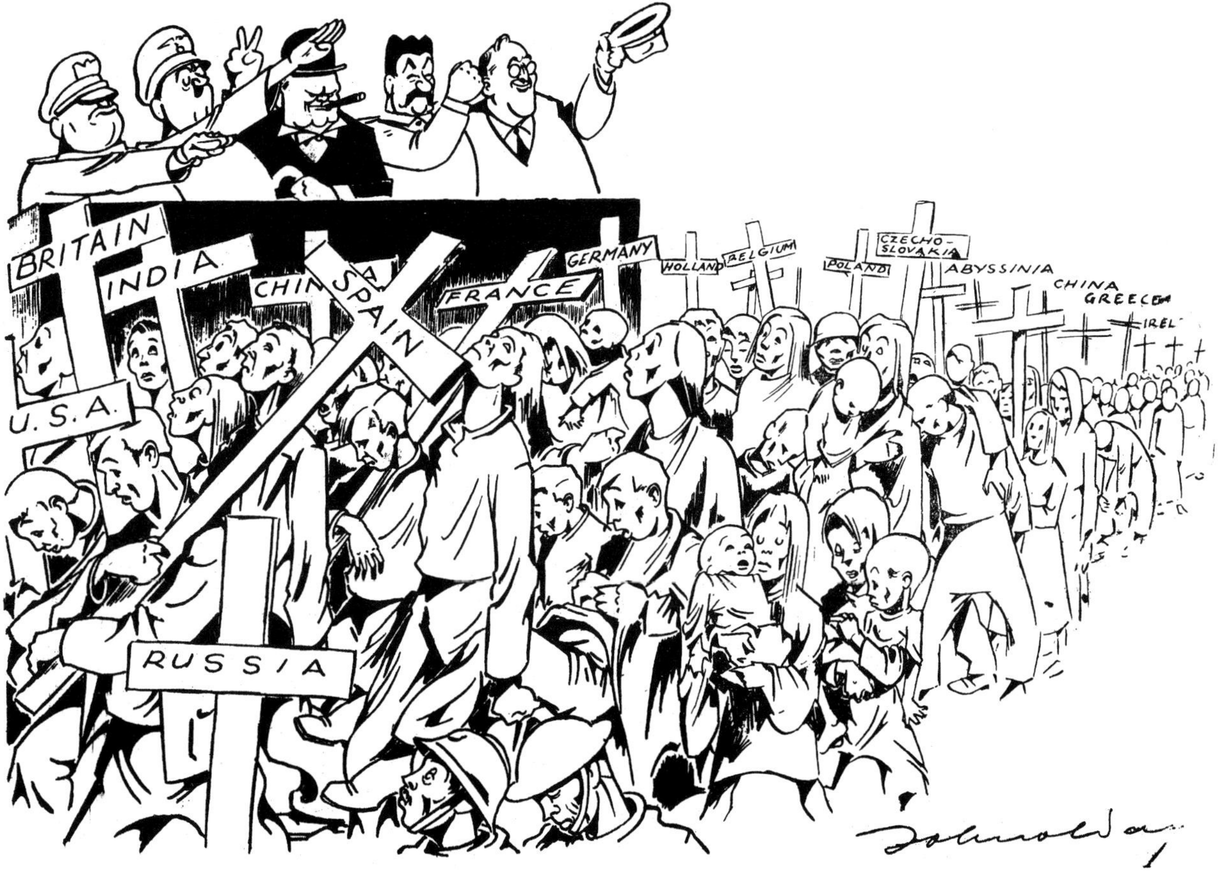
BRITAIN
INDIA
SPAIN
FRANCE
GERMANY
HOLLAND
BELGIUM
POLAND
CZECHO-SLOVAKIA
ABYSSINIA
CHINA
U.S.A.
RUSSIA

Our allies can afford the casualties in men far better than the
enemy . . .

Daily Express, 1st June 1942

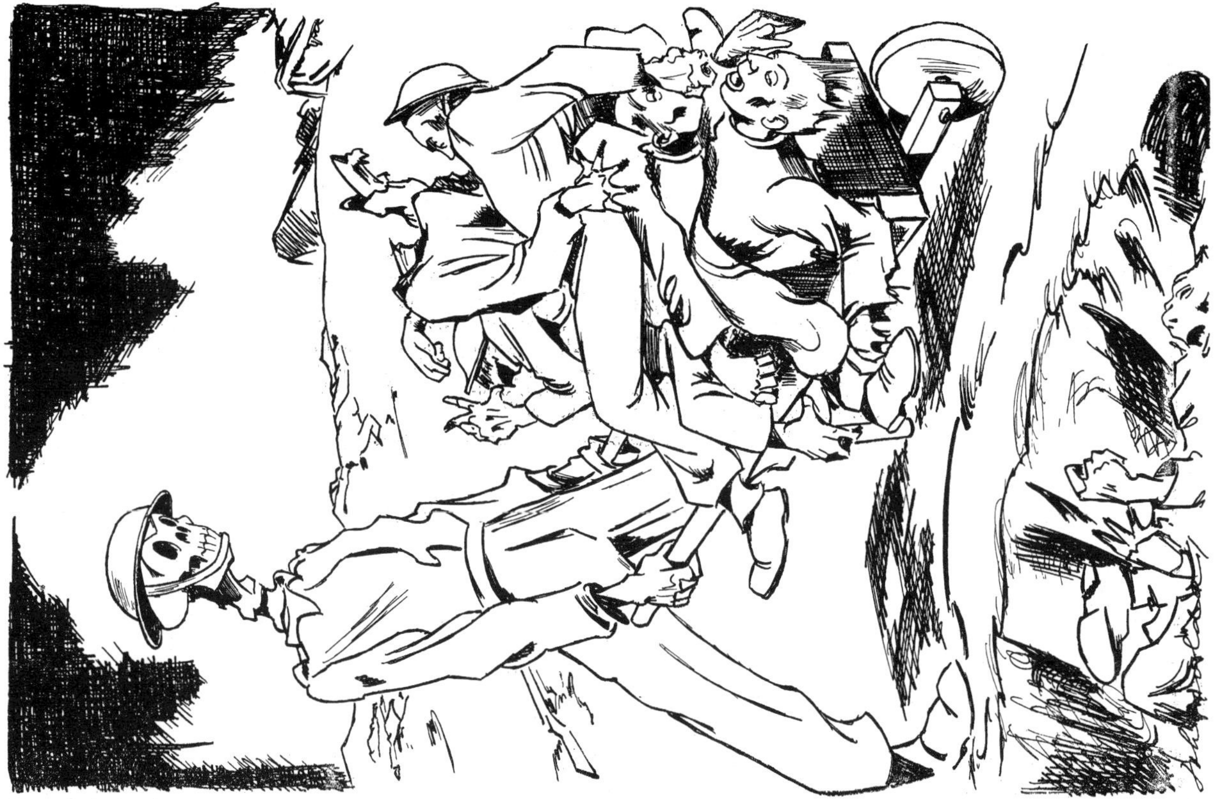

TO THE COMMON GRAVE

In the last war we did not sacrifice comfort except under duress: we earned income by service for which the labourer was worthy of his hire; we made large profits and we won the war. Victory was ours. Victory for "vested interests" together with every interest for which comfort, income, profits, and life could be preserved. Only those who sacrificed income, profits, and life went down. Only those went under. Only those lost the war.

Sir Oswald Stoll, *The Stage*, 21st November 1940

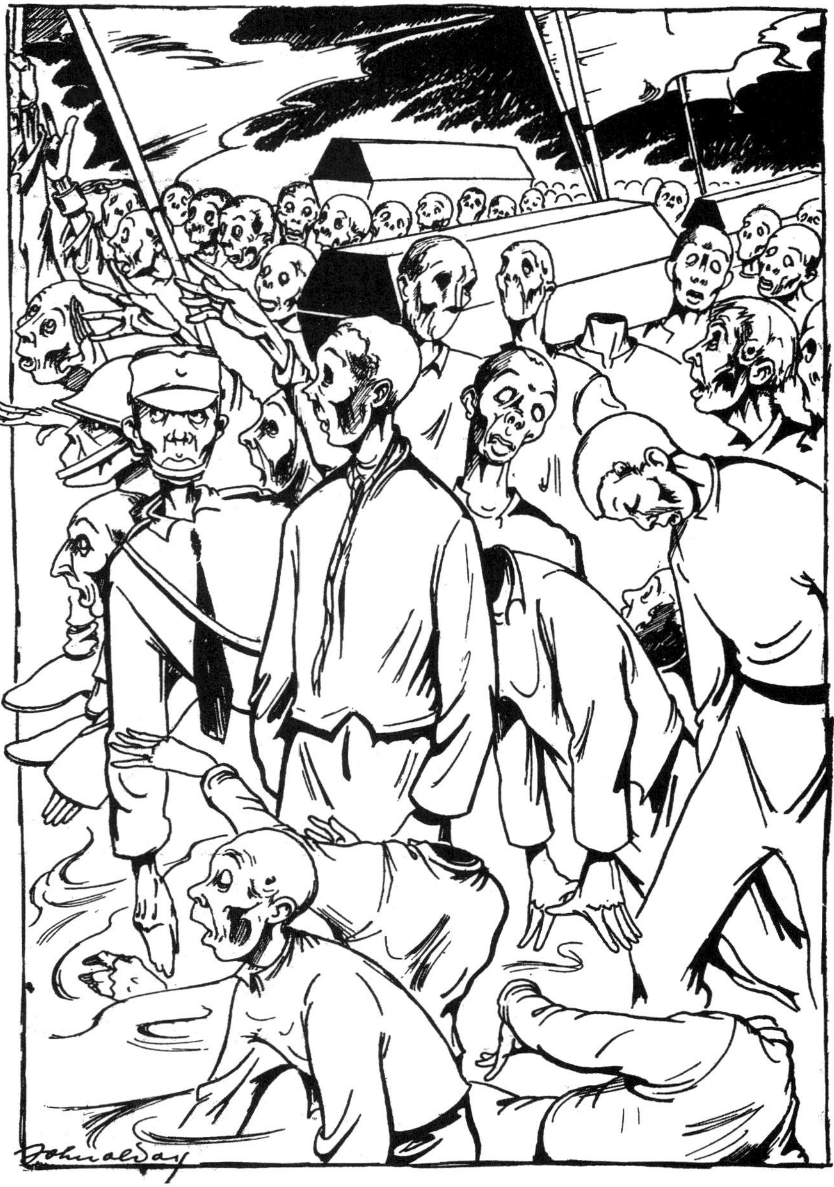
John al Day

THE PROCESSION OF THE VICTIMS

The cost of the last war:
12,996,571 dead. 16,257,000 wounded. 5,669,000 incapacitated
for life. 186,233,637,097 dollars Direct Financial Expenditure.
84,510,000,000 dollars losses in property.

Neither your country, nor humanity, neither you nor your class –
the Workers – gain anything by war. It is only the big financiers
and capitalists who profit by it.

Alexander Berkman, Now and After

YOU ARE MAKING A GOOD JOB OF IT SON!

There is no greater condemnation of our civilisation than the fact that it results in means becoming ends, while the true end, which is man himself, has become a means – no doubt a more expensive one than a dog, but cheaper than a cow or a machine gun.

Ignazio Silone, *The School for Dictators*

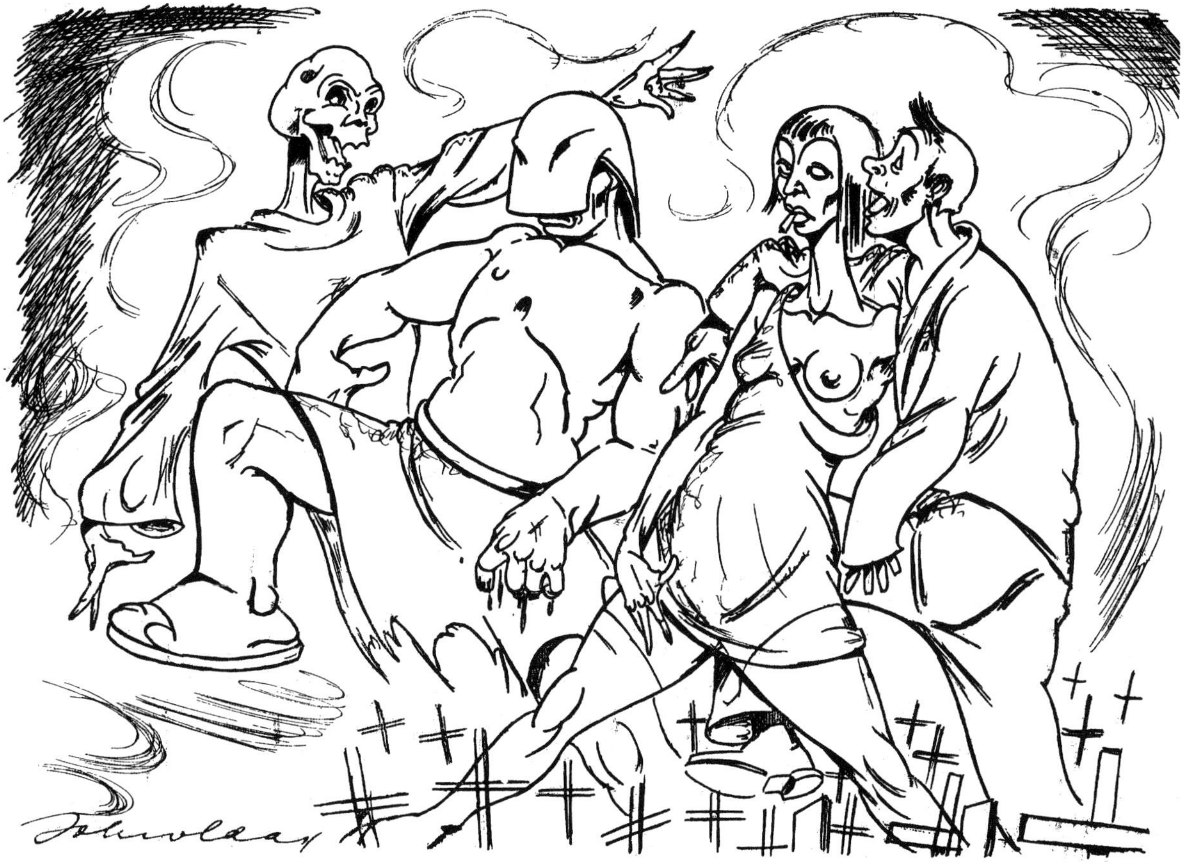

Freedom Press, founded 1886, publishes *Freedom* fortnightly, *The Raven* quarterly (number 29 is on World War II), and anarchist books and pamphlets, and sells books on anarchism wholesale and retail. A full list of publications in stock is available on request.

Some seventy Freedom Press titles are currently in print, and obtainable from bookshops or direct from Freedom Press (money with order), post free in the UK, add 15% p&p to other countries.

Two books by Marie Louise Berneri:
Journey through Utopia £4.50
Neither East nor West £4.50 (cartoons by John Olday)

Four books of cartoons by Donald Rooum, each £1.95
Wildcat Anarchist Comics
Wildcat Strikes Again
Wildcat ABC of Bosses
Health Service Wildcat

Extracts from *War Commentary*, 1938-50
World War – Cold War £6.95
The Left and World War II £1.95
British Imperialism and the Palestine Crisis £1.95

Errico Malatesta **Anarchy** £1.95
Colin Ward **Anarchy in Action** £3.00
Alexander Berkman **ABC of Anarchism** £2.00
Peter Kropotkin
    Anarchism and Anarchist Communism £1.75
Peter Kropotkin **The State: its historic role** £1.75
Rudolph Rocker
    Anarchism and Anarchosyndicalism £1.25
Various writers
    What is Anarchism? an introduction £1.95

Colin Ward **Talking Houses** £5.00
Colin Ward **Freedom to Go** £3.50
Harold Sculthorpe **Freedom to Roam** £3.50
Tony Gibson **Love, Sex and Power in Later Life** £3.50
Michael Bakunin
    Marxism Freedom and the State £1.50
Various writers **Why Work?** £4.50

Freedom Press, (in Angel Alley) 84b Whitechapel High Street, London E1 7QX. Telephone 0171 247 9249.